summer
cooking

BRIDGET JONES

using the season's finest ingredients

summer
cooking

LORENZ BOOKS

This edition is published by Lorenz Books

Lorenz Books is an imprint of Anness Publishing Ltd
Hermes House, 88–89 Blackfriars Road, London SE1 8HA
tel. 020 7401 2077; fax 020 7633 9499
www.lorenzbooks.com; info@anness.com

© Anness Publishing Ltd 2003

This edition distributed in the UK by Aurum Press Ltd,
25 Bedford Avenue, London WC1B 3AT; tel. 020 7637 3225; fax 020 7580 2469

This edition distributed in the USA and Canada by National Book Network, 4720 Boston
Way, Lanham, MD 20706; tel. 301 459 3366; fax 301 459 1705; www.nbnbooks.com

This edition distributed in Australia by Pan Macmillan Australia, Level 18, St Martins
Tower, 31 Market St, Sydney, NSW 2000; tel. 1300 135 113; fax 1300 135 103;
customer.service@macmillan.com.au

This edition distributed in New Zealand by David Bateman Ltd, 30 Tarndale Grove,
Off Bush Road, Albany, Auckland; tel. (09) 415 7664; fax (09) 415 8892

PUBLISHER: Joanna Lorenz
MANAGING EDITOR: Judith Simons
PROJECT EDITOR: Katy Bevan
DESIGNER: Adelle Morris
EDITORIAL READER: Jay Thundercliffe
PRODUCTION CONTROLLER: Joanna King
COVER PHOTOGRAPHY: Martin Brigdale
PHOTOGRAPHERS: Caroline Arber, Martin Brigdale,
Gus Filgate, Amanda Heywood, Don Last,
William Lingwood, Thomas Odulate, Craig Robertson
RECIPES: Ghillie Basan, Angela Boggiano, Matthew Drennan,
Joanna Farrow, Nicola Graimes, Lucy Knox, Sara Lewis,
Maggie Mayhew, Keith Richmond, Rena Salaman,
Anne Sheasby, Marlena Spieler, Linda Tubby,
Kate Whiteman, Jeni Wright

10 9 8 7 6 5 4 3 2 1

NOTES

Bracketed terms are intended for
American readers.

For all recipes, quantities are given in both
metric and imperial measures and, where
appropriate, measures are also given in
standard cups and spoons. Follow one set,
but not a mixture, because they are not
interchangeable.

Standard spoon and cup measures are level.
1 tsp = 5ml, 1 tbsp = 15ml, 1 cup = 250ml/8fl oz

Australian standard tablespoons are 20ml.
Australian readers should use 3 tsp in place
of 1 tbsp for measuring small quantities of
gelatine, flour, salt, etc.

Medium (US large) eggs are used unless
otherwise stated.

CONTENTS

INTRODUCTION

Summer is the season for celebrating the finest fresh ingredients. Wandering through the garden fills the senses with the scents of herbs and visually exciting produce. An abundance of fruit and vegetable shapes, colours and textures creates a wonderful display in the warm sunshine.

Events in the garden are mirrored in the marketplace, as supermarkets stack their shelves with local goods as well as fruit and vegetables from distant suppliers, and market stalls fill with a cornucopia of ingredients at affordable prices. In the summer months there is almost unlimited choice and those who are not faced with a home-grown glut of crops have to be strong-willed to resist the temptation to overstock in sheer enthusiasm for the quality of fresh foods available.

Summer style

When the weather is hot the cooking should be easy. This is not the season for spending hours standing over a hot stove – sociable dishes that make the most of quick methods and sunny days are far more fun.

Cooking outdoors on a barbecue provides the ideal opportunity for sharing the work. Everyone takes some responsibility for basting and turning tender cuts and succulent vegetables over hot coals. Whether it is in the back garden or on a beach with friends, there cannot be many better ways to eat when it is warm enough. The smallest helping hands can pass around plates if they are the shatterproof kind.

Picnics are the other perfect answer to summer eating. They can be humble or ostentatious, according to mood and occasion. Even the simplest sandwich becomes irresistible in summertime – sweet, ripe and lightly salted tomatoes are fabulous in lightly buttered, spongy fresh bread.

Today's picnickers are just as likely to pack chilled soups, marinated chargrilled vegetables and tempting savoury flans alongside traditional salads. Grand picnic hampers that were once heavily laden with pies, cold meat roasts and elaborately garnished terrines, are lightened and enlivened by modern salad fusions of fruit and vegetables with peppery leaves, handfuls of aromatic herbs and bright edible flowers. Meanwhile, glorious cheeses and oil-drizzled charcuterie are exciting and easy alternatives to intimidating pies and rich cream coatings on cold poached poultry.

Informal and fun

In the summer months formal dining can be abandoned completely to a more relaxed approach, even for special celebrations. From lazy weekend parties to summer weddings, the mood is more of soirée than silver service, with the emphasis on pre-planning to share and spread the workload, rather than a huge last-minute effort.

Summer buffets are most likely to be cold, with an eclectic selection of simple finger food or fork dishes for effortless eating. Dinner and supper parties are often centred on a salad-style main dish of hot and cold ingredients, flanked by pasta to start and fresh berries to finish. Leisurely sampling and savouring in airy surroundings replaces regimented courses served in the comforting warmth of a kitchen or dining room.

Everyday meals are light and healthy, with the focus on Mediterranean-style recipes, Asian stir-fries and fresh seafood. Several separate savouries may be eaten individually with warm bread instead of a combination of main dish, its starchy accompaniment and complementary vegetables. Fresh fruit and refreshing sorbets or ice creams are especially welcome desserts – they are also excellent snacks.

Flavours of summer

Summer takes many by surprise. One minute there is a limited harvest of tasty spring vegetables to be selected with care and the next the growing season seems to go mad. From precious quantities of young crops to overflowing basketfuls of vegetables and soft fruit – most gardeners have experienced the strange sensation of cultivating courgettes (zucchini) and aubergines (eggplant) that seem to grow before their very eyes.

Many spring vegetables continue to provide ample supplies throughout the summer, changing from baby first crop to mature produce. Salad leaves crop continuously and successive plantings ensure a steady harvest rather than sudden gluts. In a good year, huge crops of fruit and vegetables tax the creativity of most cooks. Tomatoes, strawberries and raspberries are all likely to yield huge crops in some years, and successive generations of cooks have mastered favourite methods of preserving summer produce.

SIMPLY FREEZING

Freezing is the easiest and most successful method of preserving large quantities of fresh fruit and vegetables. The most important point is to wash, dry, trim and prepare the fruit or vegetables before freezing, so that they will be ready to cook straight from frozen. Beans, berries and soft fruit are favourite freezer candidates.

Blanching is largely unnecessary – tests have shown that the difference it makes is negligible over periods of 6–9 months – but adequate packing in thick, well-sealed bags is important to keep the produce in good condition. Open freezing provides "free flow" separated items direct from the freezer. Spread fruit or beans on trays lined with baking parchment and place in the freezer. As soon as they are frozen, place into bags and seal as normal. Then you will be able to remove small amounts of fruit or beans without the pieces breaking up. Freezing large batches of soups, purées and sauces is an excellent way of preserving vegetables, like tomatoes, that don't freeze well raw.

DRYING AND SEMI-DRYING

In suitable climates, drying is a brilliant method of concentrating the flavour of vegetables such as peppers and tomatoes. When the luxury of stringing up prepared and cut vegetables to dry in the sun is not available, slowly roasting them to a concentrated semi-dried state in a barely warm oven is a good way of reducing their volume. They should be laid out on a rack and turned occasionally. Once dried and cooled, they can be packed in olive oil in sterilized jars, covered and stored in the refrigerator; alternatively, the concentrated vegetables can be frozen – ideal for adding to salads and pasta.

Drying is the traditional method of preserving herbs for winter use. While it may not be suitable for the soft-leafed varieties, as they will disintegrate, it is still a good method for some of the woody herbs, such as rosemary, sage and thyme. Wash and dry the sprigs, then hang them upside down in a warm, dry place. Enclose each bunch in a brown paper bag, tying it neatly around the stems. When the herbs are thoroughly crisp and dry they can be stored in an airtight jar in a cool, dark place.

SUMMER PRESERVES

- Jams, jellies and syrups are all ideal for soft fruit, especially currants and gooseberries, which are rich in pectin, and full-flavoured raspberries and strawberries.

- Tomatoes can be used in chutneys and ketchups.

- Flavoured vinegars are excellent made with fruit or herbs, such as raspberries, blackcurrants, peaches, basil, tarragon or chives. Use good-quality ripe fruit and perfect herbs and macerate for 2–5 days in wine vinegar or cider vinegar, crushing frequently. Strain and sweeten fruit vinegars, then pour into clean sterilized bottles and store in a cool, dark place. Use in dressings, sauces and drinks. Herb vinegars make good salad dressings and sauces, especially flavoured cider vinegar or balsamic vinegar that can be used for deglazing pan juices after cooking meat or fish.

Cool cooking

Being outdoors is the best way to make the most of summer, so smart cooks cut down on kitchen time without compromising on quality. The following are a few suggestions for achieving the best balance by following the "less is more" principle.

SOURCING THE BEST

Although nothing can better the flavour of ingredients that have come straight from the ground, food that has only been transported for a few hours is the next best thing. Fruit and vegetables that are flown halfway across the world are picked under-ripe to ensure that they still have a shelf life when they reach the supermarket. Although they may look perfect or be a regulation size, their flavour is usually lacklustre. Check the labels on packets, shelving and boxes to find food that is produced as close to home as possible.

RAW GOODNESS

Serve good produce raw as crudités, in salads or in cold uncooked soups (such as gazpacho) and fruit or vegetable juices and smoothies. This not only saves time but also results in dishes that are full of flavour, texture and vitamin goodness.

COOK AHEAD

Cooking early, in the cool of the morning, or late in the evening is a good way of avoiding hot sessions in the heat of day. Braised dishes and light casseroles can be reheated just before serving and baked or boiled ham can be left to cool and served cold. Cool the cooked food as quickly as possible, then chill it until ready to serve.

FRESH IS BEST

- Make the most of your garden, planters and hanging baskets to cultivate as much fresh produce as possible. This way you KNOW it is good.

- Buy from local growers and farmers, looking out for organic sources that mean , for the most healthy and flavoursome produce.

- Take advantage of local seafood if you live near the coast or take a cool box if you visit a port where fresh fish and shellfish are landed.

SELECTING FOR SIMPLICITY

- Fish and shellfish are light and they cook quickly.

- Light poultry, such as chicken or duck breast fillets, and tender cuts of meat cook quickly.

- The best cuts and ingredients invariably make the best end results with less fuss.

PRACTICAL PREPARATION

- Keep preparation of fresh fuit and vegetables to a minimum to preserve nutrients and time.

- Balance minimum peeling with fine cutting and slicing, so that ingredients cook quickly.

- Marinating moistens food before grilling (broiling) or cooking on a barbecue and avoids heavy sauces. Oil, fruit juice and yogurt are all excellent mediums for marinades.

LIGHT METHODS AND SHORT TIMES

- Cook fresh, finely cut produce briefly – stir-frying in the minimum oil or butter.

- Grilling, pan-frying, cooking on a barbecue and roasting for short times at a high temperature are ideal for fine cuts of fish, chicken and meat.

- Light poaching and brief simmering are good methods for fish, chicken, eggs and vegetables.

Success with summer ingredients

Here are six categories of ingredients divided by their type and the cooking and preparation methods used.

1 TENDER-SKINNED PRODUCE

The vegetable-fruits are at their best in summer. Tomatoes, cucumber, courgettes (zucchini), aubergines (eggplant) and (bell) peppers can all do without peeling.

- Select plump, firm and smooth examples that have not been bruised or battered. Wash them well and dry them on a dishtowel.
- Discard the stalk ends and cut out any tough core or stalk from tomatoes.
- Remove the seeds and pith from inside peppers.
- To remove the seeds from cucumber, cut the cucumber in half lengthways and scoop out the seeds with a teaspoon.

2 ROOTS, STEMS AND TUBERS

These usually have to be washed and trimmed and may need to be peeled, depending on the recipe. Avoid peeling to retain the best of the vitamin content which is in the skin.

- Scrub root vegetables, such as carrots, potatoes and turnips, if they are not to be peeled before cooking, and remove any "eyes" or similar marks.
- Boil beetroot (beet) in its skin. Trim off the leaf, leaving stalk and root ends in place. Slide off the skin from the freshly cooked, hot beetroot.
- Celery and fennel should be thoroughly washed to remove dirt from between the layers of stem. Cut heads of fennel in half and trim the tough core from the fennel.
- Corn can be grilled (broiled) or roasted in its outer husk but the fine silky threads should be removed first and the husk replaced around the kernels. Remove all the covering to boil the corn. To remove the kernels, cut down the outside of the cob with a sharp knife.

3 SHOOTS AND LEAVES

Wash by swirling in cold water. Do not leave them to soak. Separate the leaves and wash their bases well to remove grit and insects. Dry in a salad spinner, or on a clean dishtowel. If you are feeling energetic, swing the towel around outside.

- Leaves may be torn or finely cut according to taste, but they should be prepared as close as possible to serving, otherwise they become sad and limp.
- Beans should be washed and trimmed. Some beans have tough strings running down their sides – use a sharp knife or potato peeler to remove these. Slice beans into lengths, or cut them at a slant into long, fine strips.

4 STONE/PIT FRUIT

Stone fruit should be firm, plump and bright in colour. Hard green fruit is unripe and tasteless – leave on a sunny windowsill until ripe. Stone fruit are excellent raw or poached; larger fruit, such as peaches and nectarines, are succulent grilled (broiled) or baked. They are good in jams, jellies, syrups and vinegars.

- To peel peaches, place them in a bowl and pour in boiling water. Leave to stand for 30–60 seconds, then drain and slit the skin with the point of a knife. The skin will now peel off.

- To stone peaches, plums and apricots, cut the fruit in half, following the natural indentation. Hold one half and twist the other, then lift it off the stone. Cut the stone out of the other half.

- A cherry pitter is used to remove the pit from cherries. Place the cherry in the small cup and push the hinged spike through it, driving the pit out through the hollow base.

5 SOFT FRUITS

Look for fruit that has a good colour and is firm and ripe. These are all good raw or lightly cooked. Currants and most gooseberries are very sharp raw and are often poached and sweetened. Currants have a high pectin content and make excellent set preserves; raspberries and mulberries have a medium pectin content; strawberries have a low pectin content but they make a softly set preserve when combined with lemon juice.

- To string currants, hold the stalk in one hand and slide the prongs of a fork down the stalk.

- To hull strawberries, grasp the fruit in one hand and twist out the stalk, pulling away the long hull at the same time.

- Figs have tender skins that can be eaten or peeled away as preferred. Wash and trim off the stalk end, then cut in half or quarters, leaving the sections attached at the base.

6 SCENTS OF SUMMER

Summer is the time to cultivate soft-leafed herbs and edible flowers. French tarragon, chives, basil, flat-leaf or curly parsley, dill, sweet cicely, fennel and chervil are all excellent. Coriander (cilantro) also grows well under glass. If ground space is limited, plant in pots or window boxes, while big hanging baskets look brilliant filled with herbs.

- Preserve fresh herbs by freezing. Wash and dry the herbs, then place tender sprigs in freezer bags. It is well worth growing large batches, then freezing them for winter use.

- Basil, coriander, mint, chives, rocket (arugula) and fennel are all excellent for making pesto-style pastes. Grind the washed herbs with pine kernels and garlic, adding plenty of olive oil to make a thin paste, then store in sterilized airtight jars in the refrigerator.

- Make full use of edible flowers such as chives, thyme, courgette (zucchini) flowers, violets, nasturtiums, chrysanthemums, elderflower, lavender and rose petals. Adding them to salads brings a vivid sense of summer to the table. They can also be used in more adventurous ways, for example, in fritters, to flavour ices, drinks and sauces, and to flavour sugar.

tempting and crisp

Crisp green beans, peppers and temptingly juicy
tomatoes are all in glut at this time of year. Use
them in chilled soups and tasty appetizers.
Fresh corn is delicious spiced up with
chillies, or cooked on the barbecue smothered
in plenty of butter it is always a treat for the
kids at a family get-together.

A piquant and fresh-tasting chilled soup from the kitchens of Spain, gazpacho is as popular today as it was when first made many centuries ago.

CLASSIC GAZPACHO

INGREDIENTS
serves six

900g | 2lb ripe tomatoes, peeled and seeded

1 cucumber, peeled and roughly chopped

2 red (bell) peppers, seeded and roughly chopped

2 garlic cloves, crushed

1 large onion, roughly chopped

30ml | 2 tbsp white wine vinegar

120ml | 4fl oz | 1/2 cup olive oil

250g | 9oz | 4 1/2 cups fresh white breadcrumbs

450ml | 3/4 pint | scant 2 cups iced water

salt and freshly ground black pepper

ice cubes, to serve

for the garnish

30–45ml | 2–3 tbsp olive oil

4 thick slices bread, cut into small cubes

2 tomatoes, peeled and finely diced

1 small onion, very finely sliced

fresh flat leaf parsley, chopped

1 In a large bowl, mix the tomatoes, cucumber, peppers, garlic and onion. Stir in the vinegar, oil, breadcrumbs and water until well mixed. Pureé the mixture in a food processor or blender until almost smooth and pour into a large bowl. If the soup is too thick, add a little cold water. Add salt and pepper to taste and chill.

2 To make the garnish, heat the oil in a frying pan and add the bread cubes.

3 Cook over a medium heat for 5–6 minutes, stirring occasionally to brown evenly. Drain on kitchen paper and put into a small bowl. Place the remaining garnishing ingredients into separate bowls or on to a serving plate.

4 Ladle the gazpacho into bowls and add ice cubes to each, then serve at once. Pass around the bowls of garnishing ingredients with the soup so that they can be added to taste.

VARIATION If your guests don't like their food too spicy, you can leave out the raw onion as some find this difficult to digest. Alternatively, spice up with an extra clove of garlic and a dash of chilli sauce.

A coolly elegant dish for an *al fresco* dinner party. Use different melons to create a subtle contrast in flavour and colour. Try a combination of Charentais and Ogen or cantaloupe melon.

MELON SOUP with MINT and MELON SORBET

INGREDIENTS
serves six to eight

2.25kg | 5–5¹/₄lb very ripe melon

45ml | 3 tbsp orange juice

30ml | 2 tbsp lemon juice

mint leaves, to garnish

for the mint and melon sorbet

25g | 1oz | 2 tbsp granulated sugar

120ml | 4fl oz | ¹/₂ cup water

2.25kg | 5–5¹/₄lb very ripe melon

juice of 2 limes

30ml | 2 tbsp chopped fresh mint

1 To make the mint and melon sorbet, put the sugar and water into a pan and heat gently until the sugar dissolves. Bring to the boil and simmer for 4–5 minutes, then remove from the heat and leave to cool.

2 Halve the melon. Scrape out the seeds, then cut it into large wedges and cut the flesh out of the skin. Weigh about 1.5kg | 3–3¹/₂lb melon.

3 Purée the melon in a food processor or blender with the cooled syrup and lime juice.

4 Stir in the mint and pour the melon mixture into an ice cream maker. Churn, following the manufacturer's instructions, or until the sorbet is smooth and firm. Alternatively, pour the mixture into a suitable container and freeze until icy around the edges. Transfer to a food processor or blender and process until smooth. Repeat the freezing and processing two or three times or until smooth and holding its shape, then freeze until firm.

5 To make the chilled melon soup, prepare the melon as in step 2 and purée it in a food processor or blender. Pour the purée into a bowl and stir in the orange and lemon juice. Place the soup in the refrigerator for 30–40 minutes, but do not chill it for too long as this will dull its flavour.

6 Ladle the soup into bowls and add a large scoop of the sorbet to each. Garnish with mint leaves and serve at once.

This luxurious Middle Eastern dip is perfect for a picnic. The quantities can be varied according to taste, depending on how creamy or tart you want it to be.

BABA GHANOUSH

1 Place the aubergines directly over the flame of a gas stove or on the coals of a barbecue. Turn the aubergines fairly frequently until deflated and the skin is evenly charred. Remove from the heat with a pair of tongs.

2 Put the aubergines in a plastic bag or in a bowl and seal tightly. Leave to cool for 30–60 minutes.

3 Peel off the blackened skin from the aubergines, reserving the juices. Chop the aubergine flesh, either by hand for a textured result or in a food processor for a smooth purée. Put the aubergine in a bowl and stir in the reserved juices.

4 Add the garlic and tahini to the aubergine and stir until smooth and well combined. Stir in the lemon juice, which will thicken the mixture. If the mixture becomes too thick, add 15–30ml | 1–2 tbsp water or more lemon juice, if you like. Season with cumin and salt to taste.

5 Spoon the mixture into a serving bowl. Drizzle with olive oil and garnish with fresh coriander leaves, hot pepper sauce and olives and | or pickled cucumbers and peppers. Serve at room temperature with pitta bread or chunks of crusty French bread.

INGREDIENTS
serves two to four

1 large or 2 medium aubergines (eggplant)

2–4 garlic cloves, chopped, to taste

90–150ml | 6–10 tbsp tahini

juice of 1 lemon, or to taste

1.5ml | 1/4 tsp ground cumin, or to taste

salt

extra virgin olive oil, for drizzling

fresh coriander (cilantro) leaves, hot pepper sauce and a few olives and | or pickled cucumbers and (bell) peppers

pitta bread or chunks of crusty French bread, to serve

Keeping the husk on the corn protects the kernels and encloses the butter, so the flavours are contained. Fresh corn with husks intact are perfect, but banana leaves or a double layer of foil are also suitable.

HUSK-GRILLED CORN on the COB

1 Heat a heavy frying pan. Add the dried chillies and roast them by stirring them continuously for 1 minute without letting them scorch. Put them in a bowl with almost boiling water to cover. Use a saucer to keep them submerged, and leave them to rehydrate for up to 1 hour. Drain, remove the seeds and chop the chillies finely.

2 Place the butter in a bowl and add the chillies, lemon juice and parsley. Season to taste and mix well.

3 Peel back the husks from each cob without tearing them. Remove the silk. Smear about 30ml | 2 tbsp of the chilli butter over each cob. Pull the husks back over the cobs, ensuring that the butter is well hidden. Put the rest of the butter in a pot, smooth the top and chill to use later. Place the cobs in a bowl of cold water and leave in a cool place for 1–3 hours; longer if that suits your work plan better.

4 Prepare the barbecue, if using, or heat the grill (broiler) to its highest setting. Remove the corn cobs from the water and wrap in pairs in foil. Once the flames have died down, position a lightly oiled grill rack over the coals to heat. When the coals are medium-hot, or have a moderate coating of ash, barbecue (grill) the corn for 15–20 minutes. Remove the foil and cook them for about 5 minutes more, turning them often to char the husks a little. Serve hot, with the rest of the butter.

INGREDIENTS
serves six

3 dried chipotle chillies

250g | 9oz | generous 1 cup butter, softened

7.5ml | 1¹/₂ tsp lemon juice

45ml | 3 tbsp chopped fresh flat leaf parsley

6 corn on the cob, with husks intact

salt and ground black pepper

The sweet aniseed flavours of sweet cicely and fennel combine beautifully with the succulent tastes of the peppers, tomatoes and piquant capers. Sweet cicely leaves make an excellent garnish and they taste just like the flowers. This dish can be served as a light lunch in hot weather or as an unusual starter for a dinner party.

ROASTED PEPPERS with SWEET CICELY

INGREDIENTS
serves four

4 red (bell) peppers, halved and deseeded

8 small or 4 medium tomatoes

15ml | 1 tbsp semi-ripe sweet cicely seeds

15ml | 1 tbsp fennel seeds

15ml | 1 tbsp capers

8 sweet cicely flowers, newly opened, stems removed

60ml | 4 tbsp olive oil

crusty bread to serve

for the garnish

a few small sweet cicely leaves

8 more flowers

1 Preheat the oven to 180°C/350°F/Gas 4. Place the red pepper halves in a large ovenproof dish and set aside.

2 To skin the tomatoes, cut a cross at the base, then pour over boiling water and leave them to stand for 30 seconds to 1 minute. Cut them in half if they are of medium size.

3 Place a whole small or half a medium tomato in each half of a pepper cavity.

4 Cover with a scattering of semi-ripe sweet cicely seeds, fennel seeds and capers and about half the sweet cicely flowers. Drizzle the olive oil all over.

5 Bake in the top of the oven for 1 hour. Remove from the oven and add the rest of the flowers. Garnish with fresh sweet cicely leaves and flowers and serve with lots of crusty bread to soak up the juices.

COOK'S TIP Try adding the stems from the sweet cicely to the water in which fruit is stewed. They will add a delightful flavour and reduce the need for sugar.

VARIATION If sweet cicely is not available, this dish can also be made with a range of different herbs, although they will all impart a distinctive flavour. Celery leaves, chervil and lovage are some you might like to try.

This is a real summer favourite, using the best ripe plum tomatoes and tenderest green beans.

GREEN BEANS with TOMATOES

1 Heat the oil in a large frying pan. Add the onion and garlic and cook for about 5 minutes, until the onion is softened but not brown.

2 Add the chopped tomatoes, white wine, beans, olives and lemon juice and cook over a low heat for 20 more minutes, stirring occasionally, until the sauce is thickened and the beans are tender. Season with salt and pepper to taste and serve immediately.

COOK'S TIP Green beans need little preparation and now that they are grown without the string, you simply trim the ends. When choosing, make sure that the beans snap easily – this is a good sign of freshness.

INGREDIENTS
serves four

30ml | 2 tbsp olive oil

1 large onion, finely sliced

2 garlic cloves, finely chopped

6 large ripe plum tomatoes, peeled, seeded and coarsely chopped

150ml | 1/4 pint | 2/3 cup dry white wine

450g | 1lb runner (green) beans, sliced in half lengthways

16 pitted black olives

30ml | 2 tbsp lemon juice

salt and freshly ground black pepper

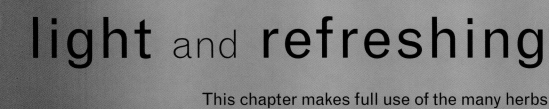

light and refreshing

This chapter makes full use of the many herbs available at this time of year – salads and light main courses for *al fresco* eating using fresh vegetables. Chives and savory, fennel, basil, parsley, oregano and dill are all used – but most can be replaced by those you have in abundance.

This combination is inspired by the Turkish tradition of eating sweet, juicy watermelon with salty white cheese in the hot summer months.

SALAD with WATERMELON and FETA CHEESE

INGREDIENTS
serves four

30–45ml | 2–3 tbsp extra virgin olive oil

juice of 1/2 lemon

5ml | 1 tsp vinegar of choice or to taste

sprinkling of fresh thyme

pinch of ground cumin

4 large slices of watermelon, chilled

1 frisée lettuce, core removed

130g | 4 1/2oz feta cheese, preferably sheep's milk feta, cut into bitesize pieces

handful of lightly toasted pumpkin seeds

handful of sunflower seeds

10–15 black olives

1 Pour the extra virgin olive oil, lemon juice and vinegar into a bowl or jug (pitcher). Add the fresh thyme and ground cumin and whisk until well combined. Set the dressing aside until you are ready to serve the salad.

2 Cut the rind off the watermelon and remove as many seeds as possible. Cut the flesh into triangular shaped chunks.

3 Put the lettuce leaves in a bowl, pour over the dressing and toss together. Arrange the leaves on a serving dish or individual plates and add the watermelon, feta cheese, pumpkin and sunflower seeds and black olives. Serve the salad immediately.

COOK'S TIP The best choice of olives for this recipe are plump black Mediterranean olives such as kalamata, other shiny, brined varieties or dry-cured black olives such as the Italian ones.

This is an Israeli dish of fresh summer vegetables and fragrant dill tossed in a rich sour cream sauce.

SUMMER SQUASH and BABY NEW POTATOES

1 Cut the squash into pieces about the same size as the potatoes. Put the potatoes in a pan and add water to cover, with the sugar and salt. Bring to the boil, then simmer for about 10 minutes – until almost tender. Add the squash and continue to cook until the vegetables are just tender, then drain.

2 Melt the butter in a large pan. Fry the spring onions until just wilted, then gently stir in the dill and vegetables.

3 Remove the pan from the heat and stir in the sour cream or yogurt. Return to the heat and stir gently until warm. Season with salt and pepper and serve.

COOK'S TIP Choose small specimens of squash with bright skins that are free from blemishes and bruises.

INGREDIENTS
serves four

400g | 14oz mixed squash, such as yellow and green courgettes (zucchini) and pale green or yellow patty pans

400g | 14oz baby new potatoes

pinch of sugar

40–75g | 1½–3oz | 3–6 tbsp butter

2 bunches spring onions (scallions), thinly sliced

1 large bunch fresh dill, finely chopped

300ml | ½ pint | 1¼ cups sour cream or Greek (US strained plain) yogurt

salt and freshly ground black pepper

This crunchy salad bursting with the flavours of fresh herbs makes an ideal light lunch or supper. Serve it with crème fraîche or yogurt cheese.

WILD GREENS and OLIVES

INGREDIENTS
serves four

1 large bunch wild rocket (arugula), about 115g | 4oz

1 large bunch mixed salad leaves

1/4 white cabbage, thinly sliced

1 cucumber, sliced

1 small red onion, chopped

2–3 garlic cloves, chopped

3–5 tomatoes, cut into wedges

1 green (bell) pepper, seeded and sliced

2–3 fresh mint sprigs, sliced or torn

15–30ml | 1–2 tbsp chopped fresh parsley and | or tarragon or dill

pinch of dried oregano or thyme

45ml | 3 tbsp extra virgin olive oil

juice of 1/2 lemon

15ml | 1 tbsp red wine vinegar

15–20 black olives

salt and freshly ground black pepper

crème fraîche or yogurt cheese, to serve

1 In a large salad bowl, put the rocket, mixed salad leaves, white cabbage, cucumber, onion and garlic. Toss gently with your fingers to combine the leaves and vegetables.

2 Arrange the tomatoes, pepper, and fresh mint, on top of the greens and vegetables. Sprinkle over the dried herbs and season. Drizzle over the oil, lemon juice and vinegar, stud with the olives and serve.

COOK'S TIP Try to find mixed salad leaves that include varieties such as lamb's lettuce, purslane and mizuna. To make yogurt cheese, mash a little feta into natural (plain) yogurt.

VARIATION Alternatively serve with cottage or cream cheese flavoured with black pepper and herbs.

Here is a risotto to celebrate the abundance of summer herbs. An aromatic blend of oregano, chives, parsley and basil combines with arborio rice to make a deliciously creamy and satisfying meal.

FRESH HERB RISOTTO

1 Cook the wild rice in boiling salted water according to the instructions on the packet, then drain and set aside.

2 Heat the butter and oil in a large, heavy pan. When the butter has melted, add the onion and cook for 3 minutes. Add the arborio rice and cook for 2 minutes, stirring to coat.

3 Pour in the dry white wine and bring to the boil. Reduce the heat and cook for 10 minutes, or until all the wine has been absorbed.

4 Add the hot vegetable stock, a little at a time, waiting for each quantity to be absorbed before adding more, and stirring continuously. After 20–25 minutes the rice should be tender and creamy. Season well.

5 Add the herbs and wild rice; heat for 2 minutes, stirring frequently. Stir in two-thirds of the Parmesan and cook until melted. Serve sprinkled with the remaining Parmesan.

COOK'S TIPS Risotto rice is essential to achieve the correct creamy texture in this dish. Other types of rice simply will not do. Fresh herbs are also a must, but you can use tarragon, chervil, marjoram or thyme instead of the ones listed here, if you prefer.

INGREDIENTS
serves four

90g | 3¹/₂oz | ¹/₂ cup wild rice

15ml | 1 tbsp butter

15ml | 1 tbsp olive oil

1 small onion, finely chopped

450g | 1lb | 2¹/₄ cups arborio rice

300ml | ¹/₂ pint | 1¹/₄ cups dry white wine

1.2 litres | 2 pints | 5 cups simmering vegetable stock

45ml | 3 tbsp chopped fresh oregano

45ml | 3 tbsp chopped fresh chives

60ml | 4 tbsp chopped fresh flat leaf parsley

60ml | 4 tbsp chopped fresh basil

75g | 3oz | 1 cup freshly grated Parmesan cheese

salt and freshly ground black pepper

This is a good first course or accompaniment, especially useful for gardeners with a glut of courgettes. You need the large ones that measure about 19cm|7¹/₂in. A barbecue with an adjustable grill is ideal for this recipe, as the wraps need to be seared quickly at the end.

WRAPS with SPINACH and MOZZARELLA

1 Prepare the barbecue or warm the grill (broiler). To make the dressing, place the garlic in a small pan with water to cover. Bring to the boil, lower the heat and simmer for 5 minutes. Drain. When cool enough to handle, pop the garlic cloves out of their skins and crush to a smooth paste with a little salt. Scrape into a bowl and add the vinegar. Whisk in the oils and season to taste.

2 Slice each courgette lengthways into six or more broad strips, about 3mm|¹/₈in wide. Lay them on a tray. Set aside 5ml|1 tsp of the oil and brush the rest over the courgette strips, evenly coating them with the oil.

3 Place a wok over a high heat. When it starts to smoke, add the reserved oil and stir-fry the spinach for 30 seconds, or until just wilted. Tip into a sieve and drain well, then pat the leaves dry with kitchen paper. Tear or slice the mozzarella balls in half and place on kitchen paper to drain.

4 Lay the courgettes on a heated, lightly oiled rack. Cook on one side only for 2–3 minutes, or until striped golden. As each strip cooks, return it to the tray, cooked-side up.

5 Place small heaps of spinach towards one end of each courgette strip. Lay two pieces of mozzarella on each pile of spinach. Season well. Use a metal spatula to transfer back to the barbecue rack and cook for about 2 minutes, or until the underside of each has golden-brown stripes. When the cheese starts to melt, fold the courgette over the filling to make a wrap. Lift off carefully and drain on kitchen paper. Serve with the garnish of salad leaves and, if wished, drizzle the dressing over the top.

INGREDIENTS
serves six

2 large yellow courgettes (zucchini), total weight about 675g | 1¹/₂lb

45ml | 3 tbsp olive oil

250g | 9oz baby leaf spinach

250g | 9oz mini mozzarella balls

salad burnet, rocket (arugula) and mizuna leaves, to garnish (optional)

salt and pepper

for the dressing

2 whole, unpeeled garlic cloves

30ml | 2 tbsp white wine vinegar

30ml | 2 tbsp olive oil

15ml | 1 tbsp extra virgin olive oil

45ml | 3 tbsp walnut oil

salt and ground black pepper

This is a light cornmeal pizza base that makes a change from the usual heavy dough. Being wheat-free it is a good recipe for anyone on a restricted diet, while also tasty enough for general consumption.

GRILLED VEGETABLE PIZZA

INGREDIENTS
serves six

1 courgette (zucchini), sliced

1 small or 2 baby aubergines (eggplant), sliced

30ml | 2 tbsp olive oil

1 yellow (bell) pepper, seeded and thickly sliced

115g | 4oz | 1 cup cornmeal

50g | 2oz | 1/2 cup potato flour

50g | 2oz | 1/2 cup soya flour

5ml | 1 tsp baking powder

2.5ml | 1/2 tsp salt

50g | 2oz | 1/4 cup soft margarine

about 105ml | 7 tbsp semi-skimmed (low fat) milk

4 plum tomatoes, skinned and chopped

30ml | 2 tbsp chopped fresh basil

115g | 4oz mozzarella cheese, sliced

salt and ground black pepper

fresh basil leaves, to garnish

1 Preheat the grill (broiler). Brush the courgette and aubergine slices with a little oil and place on a grill rack with the pepper slices. Cook under the grill until lightly browned, turning once.

2 Meanwhile, preheat the oven to 200°C | 400°F | Gas 6. Place the cornmeal, potato flour, soya flour, baking powder and salt in a mixing bowl and stir to mix. Lightly rub in the margarine until the mixture resembles coarse breadcrumbs, then stir in enough milk to make a soft but not sticky dough.

3 Place the dough on a sheet of baking parchment on a baking sheet and roll or press it out to form a 25cm | 10in round, making the edges slightly thicker than the centre.

4 Brush the pizza dough with any remaining oil, then spread the chopped tomatoes over the dough. Sprinkle with the chopped fresh basil and season with salt and pepper. Arrange the grilled vegetables over the tomatoes and top with the cheese.

5 Bake in the oven for 25–30 minutes until crisp and golden brown. Garnish the pizza with fresh basil leaves and serve immediately, cut into slices.

Infused with aromatic herbs and simple to make, this delicate flan makes a delightful lunch dish on a hot day and would be a welcome offering at a picnic.

SUMMER HERB RICOTTA FLAN

1 Preheat the oven to 180°C | 350°F | Gas 4 and lightly grease a 23cm | 9in springform cake tin (pan) with oil. Mix together the ricotta, Parmesan and egg yolks in a food processor or blender. Add the herbs and salt, and blend until smooth and creamy.

2 Whisk the egg whites in a large bowl until they form soft peaks. Gently fold the egg whites into the ricotta mixture, taking care not to knock out too much air. Spoon the ricotta mixture into the tin and smooth the top.

3 Bake for 1 hour 20 minutes or until the flan is risen and the top is golden. Remove from the oven and brush lightly with olive oil, then sprinkle with paprika. Leave the flan to cool before removing from the tin.

4 Make the tapenade. Place the olives and garlic in a food processor or blender and process until finely chopped. Gradually add the olive oil and blend to a coarse paste, then transfer to a serving bowl. Garnish the flan with fresh herb leaves and the reserved olives if wished, and serve with the tapenade.

INGREDIENTS
serves four

olive oil, for greasing and glazing

800g | 1lb 11oz | 3 1/2 cups ricotta cheese

75g | 3oz | 1 cup finely grated Parmesan cheese

3 eggs, separated

60ml | 4 tbsp torn fresh basil leaves

60ml | 4 tbsp snipped fresh chives

45ml | 3 tbsp fresh oregano leaves

2.5ml | 1/2 tsp salt

2.5ml | 1/2 tsp paprika

freshly ground black pepper

fresh herb leaves, to garnish

for the tapenade

400g | 14oz | 3 1/2 cups pitted black olives, rinsed and halved, reserving a few whole to garnish (optional)

5 garlic cloves, crushed

75ml | 5 tbsp | 1/3 cup olive oil

fresh and tasty

The last thing you need on a summer's day is to be trapped in the kitchen. Here are some quick recipes to delight family and friends, impressing without exhausting the host. Even the roast chicken could be cooked in the evening and chilled for the next day.

The aroma that wafts out of these fish parcels as you open them is deliciously tempting. If you don't like Eastern flavours, use white wine, herbs and thinly sliced vegetables, or Mediterranean ingredients such as tomatoes, basil and olives.

SALMON in a PARCEL

INGREDIENTS
serves four

2 carrots

2 courgettes (zucchini)

6 spring onions (scallions)

2.5cm | 1in piece of fresh root ginger, peeled

1 lime

2 garlic cloves, thinly sliced

30ml | 2 tbsp teriyaki marinade or Thai fish sauce

5–10ml | 1–2 tsp clear sesame oil

4 salmon fillets, about 200g | 7oz each

ground black pepper

rice, to serve

1 Cut the carrots, courgettes and spring onions into matchsticks and set them aside. Cut the ginger into matchsticks and put these in a small bowl. Using a zester, pare the lime thinly. Add the pared rind to the ginger, with the garlic.

2 Place the teriyaki marinade or Thai fish sauce into a bowl and stir in the juice from the lime and the sesame oil.

3 Preheat the oven to 220°C/425°F/Gas 7. Cut out four rounds of baking parchment, each with a diameter of 40cm/16in. Season the salmon with pepper. Lay a fillet on each paper round, about 3cm/1¼in off centre. Scatter ¼ of the ginger mixture over each and pile ¼ of the vegetable matchsticks on top. Spoon ¼ of the teriyaki marinade or Thai fish sauce mixture over the top.

4 Fold the baking parchment over the salmon and roll the edges of the parchment over to seal each parcel very tightly.

5 Place the salmon parcels on a baking sheet and cook in the oven for 10–12 minutes, depending on the thickness of the fillets. Put the parcels on plates and serve with rice.

VARIATION Thick fillets of hake, halibut, hoki and fresh or undyed smoked haddock and cod can all be used for this dish.

Sardines spiced with cumin and coriander are popular in the coastal regions of Morocco, both in restaurants and as street food. Served with the luscious salad, the only other essential ingredient is fresh crusty bread to mop up the tasty juices.

SPICED SARDINES with FENNEL SALAD

1 Rinse the sardines and pat them dry on kitchen paper, then rub inside and out with a little coarse salt.

2 In a bowl, mix the grated onion with the olive oil, cinnamon, ground roasted cumin and coriander, paprika and black pepper. Make several slashes into the flesh of the sardines and smear the onion and spice mixture all over the fish, inside and out and into the gashes. Leave the sardines to stand for about 1 hour to allow the flavours of the spices to penetrate the flesh.

3 Meanwhile, prepare the salad. Peel the grapefruits with a knife, removing all the pith then peel in neat strips down the outside of the fruit. Cut between the membranes to remove the segments of fruit intact. Cut each grapefruit segment in half, place in a bowl and sprinkle with salt.

4 Trim the fennel, cut in half lengthways and slice finely. Add the fennel to the grapefruit with the spring onions, cumin and olive oil. Toss lightly, then garnish with the olives.

5 Preheat the grill (broiler) or barbecue. Cook the sardines for 3–4 minutes on each side, basting with any leftover marinade. Sprinkle with fresh coriander and serve with lemon wedges for squeezing over and the refreshing grapefruit and fennel salad.

INGREDIENTS
serves four to six

12 fresh sardines, gutted

1 onion, grated

60–90ml | 4–6 tbsp olive oil

5ml | 1 tsp ground cinnamon

10ml | 2 tsp cumin and coriander seeds, roasted and ground

5ml | 1 tsp paprika

5ml | 1 tsp ground black pepper

coarse salt

2 lemons, cut into wedges and fresh, chopped coriander (cilantro) to serve

for the salad

2 ruby grapefruits

5ml | 1 tsp sea salt

1 fennel bulb

2–3 spring onions (scallions), finely sliced

2.5ml | 1/2 tsp ground roasted cumin

30–45ml | 2–3 tbsp olive oil

handful of black olives to garnish

Monkfish has a matchless flavour and benefits from being cooked simply. Teaming it with wilted baby spinach and toasted pine nuts is inspirational.

WARM MONKFISH SALAD

INGREDIENTS
serves four

2 monkfish fillets, about 350g | 12oz each

25g | 1oz | 1/4 cup pine nuts

15ml | 1 tbsp olive oil

15g | 1/2oz | 1 tbsp butter

225g | 8oz baby spinach leaves, washed and stalks removed

salt and freshly ground black pepper

for the dressing

5ml | 1 tsp Dijon mustard

5ml | 1 tsp sherry vinegar

60ml | 4 tbsp olive oil

1 garlic clove, crushed

1 Holding the knife at a slight angle, cut each monkfish fillet into 12 diagonal slices. Season lightly and set aside.

2 Heat a frying pan, put in the pine nuts and shake them about for a while until golden brown. Do not allow to burn. Transfer to a plate and set aside.

3 Make the dressing by whisking all the ingredients together until smooth and creamy. Pour the dressing into a small saucepan, season to taste and heat gently.

4 Heat the oil and butter in a ridged griddle or frying pan until sizzling. Add the fish and sauté for 20–30 seconds on each side.

5 Put the spinach leaves in a large bowl and pour over the warm dressing. Sprinkle on the toasted pine nuts, reserving a few, and toss together well. Divide the dressed spinach leaves among four serving plates and arrange the monkfish slices on top. Scatter the reserved pine nuts on top and serve.

VARIATION Substitute any seasonal salad leaves for the spinach, such as rocket (arugula) or mizuna.

You can vary the seafood in this Italian salad according to what is available, but try to include at least two kinds of shellfish and some squid. The salad is good warm or cold, excellent for a summer dinner party.

SEAFOOD SALAD

1 Put the mussels and clams in a large pan with the white wine. Cover and cook over a high heat, shaking the pan occasionally, for about 4 minutes, until they have opened. Discard any that remain closed. Use a slotted spoon to transfer the shellfish to a bowl, then strain and reserve the cooking liquid and set it aside.

2 Cut the squid into thin rings and chop the tentacles. Leave small squid whole. Halve the scallops horizontally.

3 Heat the oil in a frying pan and add the garlic, chilli, squid, scallops and corals. Sauté for about 2 minutes, until just cooked and tender. Lift the squid and scallops out of the pan and reserve the oil.

4 When the shellfish are cool enough to handle, shell them, keeping a dozen of each in the shell. Peel all but 6–8 of the prawns. Pour the shellfish cooking liquid into a small pan, set over a high heat and reduce by half. Mix all the shelled and unshelled mussels and clams with the squid and scallops, then add the prawns.

5 To make the dressing, whisk the mustard with the vinegar and lemon juice and season to taste. Add the olive oil, whisk vigorously, then whisk in the reserved shellfish cooking liquid and the oil from the frying pan. Pour the dressing over the seafood mixture and toss lightly to coat well.

6 Arrange the chicory and radicchio leaves around the edge of a large serving dish and pile the mixed seafood salad in the centre. Sprinkle with the chopped flat leaf parsley and serve immediately, or chill first.

INGREDIENTS
serves four to six

450g | 1lb live mussels, scrubbed and bearded

450g | 1lb small clams, scrubbed

105ml | 7 tbsp dry white wine

225g | 8oz squid, cleaned

4 large scallops, with their corals

30ml | 2 tbsp olive oil

2 garlic cloves, finely chopped

1 small dried red chilli, crushed

225g | 8oz cooked prawns (shrimp), in the shell

6–8 large chicory (Belgian endive) leaves

6–8 radicchio leaves

15ml | 1 tbsp chopped flat leaf parsley, to garnish

for the dressing

5ml | 1 tsp Dijon mustard

30ml | 2 tbsp white wine or cider vinegar

5ml | 1 tsp lemon juice

120ml | 4fl oz | 1/2 cup extra virgin olive oil

Even in the summer it is great to enjoy a roast. Rubbing the outside of the bird with lemon, smearing it generously with butter and sprinkling it with salt gives a beautiful deep brown, crisp skin, and keeps the flesh moist and succulent. The garlic roasts to a nutty, melting softness. Eat hot, or chill for a picnic treat.

ROAST CHICKEN with ROASTED GARLIC

INGREDIENTS
serves four

1.6kg | 3¹/₂lb free-range (farm-fresh) chicken

1 lemon

2 bay leaves

1 small bunch fresh thyme

50g | 2oz | ¹/₄ cup butter

4–6 garlic heads

salt and freshly ground black pepper

1 Preheat the oven to 200°C | 400°F | Gas 6. Untie any trussing and tuck the wings under the chicken. Remove any fat from the cavity. Rub the cut the lemon halves over the chicken. Tuck the lemons inside the cavity with the bay leaves and thyme. Spread the butter all over the breast and legs, seasoning well. Put the bird in a roasting pan.

2 Now prepare the garlic. Peel away some of the papery skins from each head. Lightly ease each head apart, but make sure the cloves remain attached. Sit the heads on a doubled sheet of kitchen foil and bring the foil up to form a parcel. Pour in 45ml | 3 tbsp water and close the parcel. Seal and place in the oven to roast with the chicken.

3 After 45 minutes, remove the roasting pan from the oven, lift out and open the parcel of garlic and set it on a baking dish. Return the chicken to the oven and cook for another 15 minutes, or until starting to go brown. Test the chicken to see if it is cooked, by inserting a skewer into the thickest part of the thigh. If the juices run clear, it is cooked, but if they are still pink, cook for another 10–15 minutes. Allow the bird to rest in the turned off oven for 15 minutes before carving.

4 Remove the chicken from the oven and pour any juices caught in the cavity into the pan. Serve the chicken with the cooking juices and the roasted garlic.

Pan-fried chicken, served with warm pesto, makes a deliciously quick main course. Serve with pasta or noodles and braised vegetables.

PAN-FRIED CHICKEN with PESTO

INGREDIENTS
serves four

15ml | 1 tbsp olive oil

4 skinless, boneless chicken breast portions

fresh basil leaves, to garnish

braised baby carrots and celery, to serve

for the pesto

90ml | 6 tbsp olive oil

50g | 2oz | 1/2 cup pine nuts

50g | 2oz | 2/3 cup freshly grated Parmesan cheese

50g | 2oz | 1 cup fresh basil leaves

15g | 1/2oz | 1/4 cup fresh parsley

2 garlic cloves, crushed

salt and freshly ground black pepper

1 Heat the oil in a frying pan. Add the chicken breast portions and cook gently for 15–20 minutes, turning several times until they are tender, lightly browned and thoroughly cooked.

2 Meanwhile, make the pesto. Place the olive oil, pine nuts, Parmesan cheese, basil leaves, parsley, garlic and seasoning in a blender or food processor. Process until mixed well together and the required texture is achieved.

3 When cooked remove the chicken from the pan, cover and keep hot. Reduce the heat slightly, then add the pesto to the pan and cook gently for a few minutes, stirring constantly, until the pesto has warmed through.

4 Pour the warm pesto over the chicken and garnish with basil leaves. Serve with braised baby carrots and celery.

This is a very easy dish to make and looks extremely impressive, and is great for entertaining as you can get several tenderloins on a barbecue. Serve with a chickpea salad topped with finely chopped onions and parsley, and flavoured with a really mustardy dressing.

BASIL and PECORINO STUFFED PORK

1 Make a 1cm|1/2in slit down the length of one of the tenderloins. Continue to slice, cutting along the fold of the meat, until you can open it out flat. Lay between two sheets of baking parchment and pound with a rolling pin to an even thickness of about 1cm|1/2in. Lift off the top sheet of parchment and brush the meat with a little oil. Press half the basil leaves on to the surface, then scatter over half the Pecorino cheese and chilli flakes. Add a little pepper.

2 Roll up lengthways to form a sausage and tie with kitchen string (twine). Repeat with the second tenderloin. Put them in a shallow bowl with the remaining oil, cover and put in a cool place until ready to cook.

3 Prepare the barbecue. Twenty minutes before you are ready to cook, season the meat with salt. Wipe any excess oil off the meat. Once the flames have died down, rake the hot coals to one side and insert a drip tray flat beside them so that the cooking temperature can be varied. Position a lightly oiled rack over the coals to heat.

4 When the coals are hot, or with a light coating of ash, put the tenderloins on to the grill rack over the coals. Cook for 5 minutes over the coals, turning to sear on all sides, then move them over the drip tray and cook for 15 minutes more. Cover with a lid or tented heavy-duty foil, and turn them over from time to time. When done, remove and wrap in foil. Leave to rest for 10 minutes before slicing into rounds and serving.

COOK'S TIP If you don't use a lid and drip tray, move the coals so these are less on one side than the other. Move the pork frequently during cooking to prevent burning.

INGREDIENTS
serves six to eight

2 pork tenderloins, each about 350g|12oz

45ml|3 tbsp olive oil

40g|1 1/2oz|1 1/2 cups fresh basil leaves, chopped

50g|2oz Pecorino cheese, grated

2.5ml|1/2 tsp chilli flakes

salt and freshly ground black pepper

Known as souvlakia, this used to be street food par excellence in Athens. Lamb makes the best souvlakia but in Greece this has now largely been replaced by pork, which is considerably cheaper. Serve with a large tomato salad and crusty bread.

SKEWERED LAMB

1 Ask your butcher to trim the meat and cut it into 4cm|1½in cubes. A little fat is desirable with souvlakia, as it keeps them moist and succulent during cooking. Separate the onion quarters into pieces, each composed of two or three layers, and slice each pepper quarter in half widthways.

2 Put the oil, lemon juice, garlic and herbs in a large bowl. Season with salt and pepper and whisk well to combine. Add the meat cubes, stirring to coat them in the mixture.

3 Cover the bowl tightly and leave to marinate for 4–8 hours in the refrigerator, stirring several times.

4 Lift the meat cubes, reserving the marinade, and thread them on long metal skewers, alternating each piece of meat with a piece of pepper and a piece of onion. Lay them across a grill (broiling) pan or baking tray and brush them with the reserved marinade.

5 Preheat a grill (broiler) until hot or prepare a barbecue. Cook the souvlakia under a medium to high heat or over the hot coals for 10 minutes, until they start to get scorched. If using the grill, do not place them too close to the heat source. Turn the skewers over, brush them again with the marinade (or a little olive oil) and cook them for 10–15 minutes more. Serve immediately.

COOK'S TIPS If you are cooking the souvlakia on a barbecue you may need to cook them for slightly longer, depending on the intensity of the heat.

INGREDIENTS
serves four

1 small shoulder of lamb, boned and with most of the fat removed

2–3 onions, preferably red onions, quartered

2 red or green (bell) peppers, quartered and seeded

75ml|5 tbsp extra virgin olive oil

juice of 1 lemon

2 garlic cloves, crushed

5ml|1 tsp dried oregano

2.5ml|½ tsp dried thyme or some sprigs of fresh thyme, chopped

salt and freshly ground black pepper

salad leaves and chillies to serve

This traditional Thai dish – known as yam nua yang – is a great way to liven up a salad. Serve as a light main course on a sultry evening in the garden.

THAI BEEF SALAD

INGREDIENTS
serves four

675g | 1½lb fillet steak (beef tenderloin) or rump (round) steak

30ml | 2 tbsp olive oil

2 small mild red chillies, seeded and sliced

225g | 8oz | 3¼ cups shiitake mushrooms, sliced

for the dressing

3 spring onions (scallions), finely chopped

2 garlic cloves, finely chopped

juice of 1 lime

15–30ml | 1–2 tbsp fish or oyster sauce

5ml | 1 tsp soft light brown sugar

30ml | 2 tbsp chopped fresh coriander (cilantro)

to serve

1 cos or romaine lettuce, torn into strips

175g | 6oz cherry tomatoes, halved

5cm | 2in piece cucumber, peeled, halved and thinly sliced

45ml | 3 tbsp toasted sesame seeds

1 Preheat the grill (broiler) until hot, then cook the steak for 2–4 minutes on each side, depending on how well done you like it. (In Thailand, the beef is traditionally served quite rare.) Leave to cool for at least 15 minutes.

2 Use a very sharp knife to slice the meat as thinly as possible and place the slices in a bowl.

3 Heat the olive oil in a small frying pan. Add the red chillies and the sliced mushrooms and cook for 5 minutes, stirring occasionally. Turn off the heat and add the grilled (broiled) psteak slices to the pan, then stir well to coat the slices in the chilli and mushroom mixture.

4 Mix all the ingredients for the dressing together in a bowl, then pour over the meat mixture and toss gently.

5 Arrange the salad ingredients on a serving plate. Spoon the warm steak mixture in the centre and sprinkle the sesame seeds over. Serve at once.

VARIATION If you can find them, yellow chillies make a colourful addition to this dish. Substitute one for one of the red chillies. This warm salad method works well whatever the green leaves you have to hand.

sweet and fruity

There are so many flowers and herbs to scent
and flavour food at this verdant time of year.
Try the heady taste of lavender, flavour with
elderflowers or decorate with rose petals.
There is something very satisfying in using
produce from your own, or someone else's, garden.

Rosewater-scented cream and fresh raspberries form the filling for this delectable dessert. Though they look impressive, these shortcakes are easy to make.

RASPBERRY and ROSE PETAL SHORTCAKES

INGREDIENTS
serves six

115g | 4oz | 1/2 cup unsalted (sweet) butter, softened

50g | 2oz | 1/4 cup caster (superfine) sugar

1/2 vanilla pod, split, seeds reserved

115g | 4oz | 1 cup plain (all-purpose) flour, plus extra for dusting

50g | 2oz | 1/3 cup semolina

icing (confectioners') sugar, for dusting

for the filling

300ml | 1/2 pint | 1 1/4 cups double (heavy) cream

15ml | 1 tbsp icing (confectioners') sugar

2.5ml | 1/2 tsp rosewater

450g | 1lb | 4 cups raspberries

for the decoration

12 miniature roses, unsprayed

6 mint sprigs

1 egg white, beaten

caster sugar (superfine), for dusting

1 Cream the butter, caster sugar and vanilla seeds in a bowl until pale and fluffy. Sift the flour and semolina together, then gradually work the dry ingredients into the creamed mixture to make a biscuit dough. Gently knead the dough on a lightly floured surface until smooth. Roll out quite thinly and prick all over with a fork. Using a 7.5cm | 3in fluted cutter, cut out 12 rounds. Place these on a baking sheet and chill for 30 minutes.

2 Meanwhile, make the filling. Whisk the cream with the icing sugar until soft peaks form. Fold in the rosewater and chill until required.

3 Preheat the oven to 180°C | 350°F | Gas 4. To make the decoration, paint the roses and mint leaves with the egg white. Dust with sugar and dry on a wire rack.

4 Bake the shortcakes for 15 minutes or until lightly golden. Lift them off the baking sheet with a metal spatula and cool on a wire rack.

5 To assemble the shortcakes, spoon the rosewater cream on to half the biscuits. Add a layer of raspberries, then top with a second shortcake. Dust with icing sugar. Decorate with the frosted roses and mint sprigs.

COOK'S TIP For best results, serve the shortcakes as soon as possible after assembling them, otherwise they are likely to turn soggy from the berries' liquid.

VARIATIONS Other soft red summer berries, such as mulberries, loganberries and tayberries would be equally good in this dessert.

Desserts don't come much easier than this – fresh figs in crisp filo pastry, with a creamy almond batter. The tart tastes wonderful served with cream or yogurt.

FRESH FIG FILO TART

1 Preheat the oven to 190°C | 375°F | Gas 5. Grease a 25 x 16cm | 10 x 6¼in baking tin (pan) with butter. Brush each filo sheet in turn with melted butter and use to line the tin.

2 Trim the excess pastry, leaving a little overhanging the edge. Arrange the figs over the base of the tart.

3 Sift the flour into a bowl and stir in the caster sugar. Add the eggs and a little of the milk and whisk until smooth. Gradually whisk in the remaining milk and the almond essence. Pour the batter over the figs.

4 Bake for 1 hour or until the batter has set and is golden. Remove the tart from the oven and allow it to cool in the tin on a wire rack for 10 minutes. Dust with the icing sugar and serve with cream, yogurt or large scoops of fresh vanilla flavoured ice cream.

INGREDIENTS
serves six to eight

5 sheets of filo pastry, each measuring 35 x 25cm | 14 x 10in, thawed if frozen

25g | 1oz | 2 tbsp butter, melted

6 fresh figs, cut into wedges

75g | 3oz | ¾ cup plain (all-purpose) flour

75g | 3oz | 6 tbsp caster (superfine) sugar

4 eggs

450ml | ¾ pint | scant 2 cups creamy milk

2.5ml | ½ tsp almond essence (extract)

15ml | 1 tbsp icing (confectioners') sugar, for dusting

whipped cream, Greek (strained plain) yogurt or vanilla ice cream, to serve

This fresh fruit salad, with its special colour and exotic flavour, is a refreshing way to end a meal. It is a great dish to serve on a day when it is too hot to cook.

SCENTED RED and ORANGE FRUIT SALAD

INGREDIENTS
serves four to six

350–400g | 12–14oz | 3–3$^{1}/_{2}$ cups strawberries, hulled and halved

3 oranges, peeled and segmented

3 small blood oranges, peeled and segmented

1–2 passion fruit

120ml | 4fl oz | $^{1}/_{2}$ cup dry white wine

sugar, to taste

1 Put the strawberries and oranges into a serving bowl. Halve the passion fruit and spoon the flesh into the bowl.

2 Pour the wine over the fruit and add sugar to taste. Toss gently and then chill until ready to serve.

VARIATIONS Other fruits that can be added include pear, kiwi fruit and banana. Tropical fruits like pomegranate or slices of starfruit add a decorative touch.

Take advantage of the short apricot season by making this charming apricot and almond dessert, delicately scented with lemon juice and orange flower water.

APRICOTS with ALMOND PASTE

1 Preheat the oven to 180°C | 350°F | Gas 4. Place the sugar, lemon juice and water in a small pan and bring to the boil, stirring occasionally until the sugar has all dissolved. Simmer gently for 5–10 minutes to make a thin syrup.

2 Place the ground almonds, icing sugar, orange flower water, butter and almond essence in a bowl and blend together to make a smooth paste.

3 Wash the apricots and then make a slit in the flesh and ease out the stone (pit). Take small pieces of the almond paste, roll into balls and press one into each of the apricots.

4 Arrange the stuffed apricots in a shallow ovenproof dish and carefully pour the sugar syrup around them. Cover with foil and bake in the oven for 25–30 minutes.

5 Serve the apricots with a little of the syrup and decorated with sprigs of fresh mint.

COOK'S TIP Always use a heavy pan when making syrup and stir constantly with a wooden spoon until the sugar has completely dissolved. Do not let the liquid come to the boil before it has dissolved, or the result will be grainy.

INGREDIENTS
serves six

75g | 3oz | 6 tbsp caster (superfine) sugar

30ml | 2 tbsp lemon juice

300ml | 1/2 pint | 1 1/4 cups water

115g | 4oz | 1 cup ground almonds

50g | 2oz | 1/2 cup icing (confectioners') sugar

a little orange flower water

25g | 1oz | 2 tbsp unsalted (sweet) butter, melted

2.5ml | 1/2 tsp almond essence (extract)

900g | 2lb fresh apricots

fresh mint sprigs, to decorate

No book of summer cooking would be complete without this well-loved, classic recipe. Although easy to make it is always an impressive centrepiece.

SUMMER PUDDING

INGREDIENTS
serves four to six

8 x 1cm | 1/2in thick slices of day-old white bread, crusts removed

800g | 1³/₄lb | 6–7 cups mixed berry fruit, such as strawberries, raspberries, blackcurrants, redcurrants and blueberries

50g | 2oz | 1/4 cup golden caster (superfine) sugar

lightly whipped double (heavy) cream or crème fraîche, to serve

1 Trim a slice of bread to fit in the base of a 1.2 litre | 2 pint | 5 cup bowl, then trim another 5–6 slices to line the sides of the bowl.

2 Place all the fruit in a pan with the sugar. Cook gently for 4–5 minutes until the juices begin to run – it will not be necessary to add any water. Allow the mixture to cool slightly, then spoon the berries and enough of their juices to moisten into the bread-lined bowl. Save any leftover juice to serve with the dessert.

3 Fold over the excess bread, then cover the fruit with the remaining bread slices, trimming them to fit. Place a small plate or saucer directly on top, fitting it inside the bowl. Weight it with a 900g | 2lb weight if you have one, or use a couple of full cans.

4 Leave the bowl in the refrigerator for at least 8 hours or overnight. To serve, run a knife between the dessert and the bowl and turn it out on to a plate. Spoon any reserved juices over the top and serve with whipped cream or crème frâiche.

Delicately perfumed with just a hint of lavender, this delightful, pastel pink sorbet is perfect for a special occasion dinner.

STRAWBERRY and LAVENDER SORBET

INGREDIENTS
serves six

150g | 5oz | 3/4 cup caster (superfine) sugar

300ml | 1/2 pint | 1 1/4 cups water

6 fresh lavender flowers

500g | 1 1/4lb | 5 cups strawberries, hulled

1 egg white

lavender flowers, to decorate

1 Put the sugar and water into a pan and gently bring to the boil, stirring constantly until the sugar has completely dissolved. Take the pan off the heat, add the lavender flowers leaving to infuse (steep) for 1 hour. Strain and, if time permits, chill the syrup before using.

2 Purée the strawberries in a food processor or in batches in a blender, then press the purée through a large sieve into a bowl.

3 BY HAND: Spoon the purée into a plastic tub or similar freezerproof container, mix in the lavender syrup and freeze for 4 hours, or until the mixture is mushy.
USING AN ICE CREAM MAKER: Pour the strawberry purée into the bowl of an ice cream maker and mix in the lavender syrup. Churn for 20 minutes, or until the mixture is thick.

4 Whisk the egg white until it just turns frothy.
BY HAND: Scoop the sorbet from the tub into a food processor, process it until smooth, then add the egg white. Spoon the sorbet back into the tub and freeze for 4 hours, or until firm.
USING AN ICE CREAM MAKER: Add the egg white to the ice cream maker and continue to churn until the sorbet is firm enough to scoop.

5 Serve the sorbet in scoops, decorated with lavender flowers.

COOK'S TIP The size of lavender flowers varies. If they are very small, you may need to use eight instead of six. To double check, taste a little of the cooled lavender syrup. If you think the flavour is a little mild, add 2–3 more flowers, reheat and cool again before using.

A classic combination that makes a really refreshing sorbet. Make it in summer as a stunning finale to an *al fresco* meal.

GOOSEBERRY and ELDERFLOWER SORBET

1 Put 30ml | 2 tbsp of the sugar in a pan with 30ml | 2 tbsp of the water. Set aside. Mix the remaining sugar and water in a separate heavy pan. Heat gently, stirring occasionally, until the sugar has dissolved. Bring to the boil and boil for 1 minute, without stirring, to make a syrup.

2 Remove from the heat and add the elderflower heads, pressing them into the syrup with a wooden spoon. Leave to infuse (steep) for about 1 hour.

3 Strain the elderflower syrup through a sieve placed over a bowl. Set the syrup aside. Add the gooseberries to the pan containing the reserved sugar and water. Cover and cook very gently for about 5 minutes, until the gooseberries have softened.

4 Transfer to a food processor or blender and add the apple juice. Process until smooth, then press through a sieve into a bowl. Leave to cool. Stir in the elderflower syrup and green food colouring. Chill until very cold.

5 BY HAND: Pour the mixture into a shallow container and freeze until thick, preferably overnight.
USING AN ICE CREAM MAKER: Churn the mixture until it holds its shape. Transfer to a freezerproof container and freeze for several hours or overnight.

6 To decorate the serving glasses, put a little egg white in a shallow bowl and a thin layer of caster sugar on a flat plate. Dip the rim of each glass in the egg white, then the sugar, to coat evenly. Leave to dry. Scoop the sorbet carefully into the glasses, decorate with elderflowers and serve.

INGREDIENTS
serves six

150g | 5oz | 2/3 cup caster (superfine) sugar

175ml | 6fl oz | 1/4 cup water

10 elderflower heads

500g | 1 1/4 lb | 4 cups gooseberries

200ml | 7fl oz | scant 1 cup apple juice

dash of green food colouring (optional)

a little beaten egg white and caster sugar, to decorate

INDEX